MAKE YOUR OWN
Outdoor Flags & Banners

Marsha McCloskey & Linda Moore

INTRODUCTION 2

1. GETTING STARTED
Make a Flag Plan 4
Prepare a Paper Pattern 8
Materials, Supplies and Tools 10

2. MAKING THE FLAG
Construct the Background Panel 12
Transfer the Design Outlines 14
Set up Machine for Zigzag Stitching 14
Reversible Appliqué 16
Appliqué Letters and Numbers 18
Headings and Grommets 20
Finishing Touches 20

3. FLAG DISPLAY AND CARE
Flag Display 21
Flag Care 23

RESOURCE GUIDE 24

INTRODUCTION

So. You have this great idea for a flag or banner. Your neighborhood pond has swans in the summer and you want a Swan Flag to hang on the deck. Or, your daughter's soccer team needs a banner to hang on the fence during games. Or, you are a quilter and you want a nautical flag with a quilt block motif for the family sailboat. Perhaps, your store could use a series of flags to spruce things up a bit and attract more customers.

We use flags to tell people who we are, what groups we belong to, and where we can be found. Brightly-colored flags flying in the wind lend excitement to an event and give the impression that "something interesting is happening here." Flags promote ideas, advertise products, and commemorate the large or small events in our lives. Decorative flags on homes call out the seasons and reflect the personalities of the people who live there.

You can buy a mass-produced flag with standard imagery for about the price of a hardcover novel. Flags with more personal messages or imagery must be custom made. If you have a generous budget, you can have a professional flagmaker make a flag to your own specifications. However, if you have basic sewing machine skills, you can make your own flag. We will tell you how.

We begin with a section called GETTING STARTED to help you plan a flag to fit your needs. Here you will learn how to design a good flag, how to prepare a full-size paper pattern, and gather the needed tools and materials. The next section, MAKING THE FLAG, presents step-by-step instructions for cutting, stitching and finishing.

The last section of this book, FLAG DISPLAY AND CARE, describes different ways to hang flags, the necessary hardware, and how to care for a flag to make it last longer. On the last page, you will find a RESOURCE GUIDE to help you find design inspiration, quality materials and hardware.

This book is for the do-it-yourself flagmaker who has a great flag idea and needs help bringing it to life.

Is it a Flag or a Banner?

Flag

Banner

FLAGS are designed and constructed to fly out and away from a pole. Dependent on the wind or movement for display, they are traditionally simple in design and carry bold symbols that can be easily seen from a distance. To maintain light weight for flyability, embellishments and extra layers are kept to a minimum.

BANNERS are designed to hang straight down so that they show "full face," and can better accommodate detailed embellishments such as words or messages.

In current usage these terms are frequently used interchangeably. For simplicity's sake, in this book, we simply say "flag."

1. GETTING STARTED

Your flag idea is probably already bubbling around in your head. You may be working with a "ready-made" design such as a school or team logo. You may only have a general idea of the kind of images you want on your flag. It may be helpful to browse through flag books (see Resource Guide on page 24) to get an idea of the colors, scale and graphics in existing flag layouts.

A "good" flag design is one that is easily recognized from a distance, gets the message across to its intended audience, and is reasonably easy to sew. For the most part, spare, simple motifs carefully arranged in two or three colors are very effective. Traditional flags are made in an array of shapes and sizes ranging from small triangular pennants to thirty-foot streamers. However, we have limited this booklet to basic rectangular flags, partly due to space considerations, and partly to keep the beginner from getting bogged down in technical details. Our aim is to provide an introduction to flagmaking. More advanced or adventuresome sewers can adapt our basic techniques to their own creative projects. Topics and flagmaking techniques we will not cover in this short booklet include: hot cutting, overlapping and flat-felled seams, fancy borders, designs that "bleed" off the edge of the flag, and complex flag shapes that require facings.

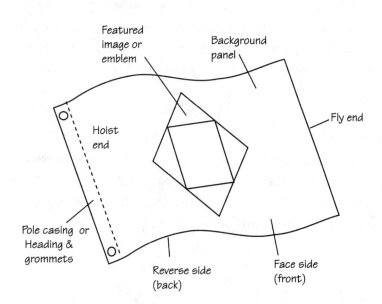

Parts of a Flag

Flag Size

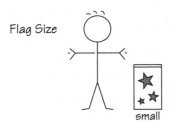
small

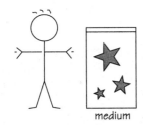
medium

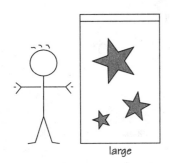
large

The total area of a flag and the size of the design increase <u>twice</u> as fast as its linear dimensions.

A **small flag** (less than 2' x 3', or 6 square feet) is for small spaces or intimate viewing, and can be made in a half or full day of sewing.

A **medium-size flag** (around 3' x 5', or 15 square feet) can easily be a major project, especially if lettering is included. Plan on a full day or two for completion.

A **large flag** or banner (4' x 6' and over, or 24 square feet) will take significantly more time. It will seem much bigger than you are while you work on it, and will require some action akin to wrestling on your part during fabrication.

MAKE A FLAG PLAN

The first step in creating a flag is to make a simple layout of the design. This Flag Plan, in the form of a full-size paper pattern, will contain all the nitty-gritty details you will need to refer to as the project progresses. These include cut <u>and</u> finished dimensions, allowances for hems and casings, design shapes, colors, and fabric requirements.

To begin, make small sketches of your flag ideas on paper. Don't worry about getting it exactly right the first time. Have fun and use your imagination to make a series of drawings. Use pencil, colored markers, or paper shape cutouts to lay out major images and design elements. Comparing various options can help you visualize how the design will look. Experiment with color, light and dark, height and width proportions, and wording, if any. Ordinary graph paper will allow you to make your drawing to scale and will help you judge the relative proportions of the shapes in the design. If you have access to a computer, graphics or drawing programs are wonderful for this process. Your sketches will eventually crystallize into a Flag Plan, so while you are sketching, here are a few things to keep in mind:

★ BIG PICTURE: Think of your flag in terms of viewing at a distance greater than a few feet. Viewed from across the room or across the street, bold colors and strong design take over and small details do not even show.

★ DISPLAY: Where and how will the flag be displayed? Do you want it to hang straight down from a dowel, or fly freely in the breeze from a flag pole? What are your display options? Do you need to take existing hardware into account? (See Flag Display, page 21.)

★ PROPORTIONS: A good starting place for laying out rectangular flags is to make the length roughly 50% longer than the height of the flag. This proportion is used in many national and state flags. Generally, in traditional flags, the featured design is approximately two-thirds to three-fourths of the height of the flag or the width of the banner.

★ SHAPES: The silhouette of a shape is what "reads" at a distance. The less fussy the better. Clean lines are easier for the viewer to interpret and will be easier to sew. If you do not like your own drawings, refer to books of copyright-free Clip Art (Dover has dozens) or children's coloring books* for simple, clear images that will convey your meaning. Remember that realistic images are not always necessary. You can substitute symbolic or abstract images. Look at flag books to see what has already been done. Use your research both for inspiration and to avoid unfortunate similarities between your flag image and symbols used for ideologies that you may want to avoid.

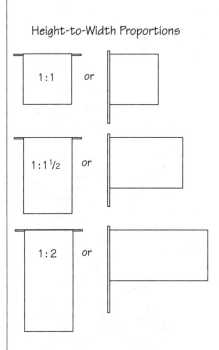

Height-to-Width Proportions

1:1 or

1:1½ or

1:2 or

As a representation of tulips the design on the right would be much easier to sew <u>and</u> to recognize from a distance.

* NOTE: Honor copyrights and trademarks on the images you choose. Make sure you have permission. You could get in trouble with some commercial images, such as Mickey Mouse or Raggedy Ann, because they are trademarked and cannot be used except by the company that owns them.

MAKE YOUR OWN Outdoor Flags & Banners

Contrast

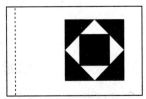

Good contrast of light and dark makes a design "read."

SEWING TIP: If your stitches are not very even, use thread that matches the background panel, then uneven stitches will blend in and not show.

FLAGMAKER'S TIP: To get a better idea of how your flag will look and how much work it will take, make a small experimental "mock-up" flag out of your selected fabrics.

★ COLOR: Readability depends on highly contrasting values and colors. In general, use only two or three colors for the best effect. The main panel of the flag will be the **background color** and the images and lettering will be **accent colors**.

Flag fabric, nylon oxford, comes in a broad range of clear, bright colors that really come to life in sunlight. These translucent colors look significantly different on the roll in the store than they do in natural lighting. Hold a swatch of each color up to natural light to see how it will look outdoors, as well as how it will look with the other colors you will be using.

Thread color is an integral part of the flag design and will affect the look of the flag. Thread that matches the color of the background panel just blends in. However, black, or contrasting thread, creates a "drawn" line effect that when seen up-close emphasizes the edges of each sewn section. The effect you choose for the front of your flag (the "best side"), will be the opposite on the reverse side. In any case, thread color is usually not discernible when a flag is viewed from a distance.

★ DURABILITY: How long does your flag need to last? How long will it be on display? Does it need to be extra tough, or just quick and easy to make? Will it be a working flag, or is it just for a onetime show? For flags that will be flown outside over a long period of time, durable construction should be a primary consideration. For indoor flags and flags that will be flown outside for only one day, by all means take shortcuts.

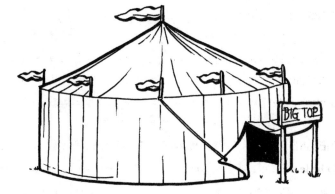

For a great effect, display several flags of the same design, color, size or shape.

★ LETTERING: Because the design shows on both the front and back of a flag, text or other directional design elements can be a special challenge. When sewn using the Reversible Appliqué method (page 16), the message on the front of the flag will appear reversed on the back of the flag.

Making crisp, polished-looking letters is time-consuming and takes substantial attention to detail. It can be much easier in the long run to find a simple clip-art image that loosely represents your idea, than to spell out the name of your event or group. Remember, every single letter has to be transferred to the fabric, cut out, and stitched onto the flag. For some perspective on the matter try this process out with a single letter. For tips and techniques on sewing letters and numbers, see page 18.

Words and letters are best for advertising, signs or a specific message (e.g. business name, event, etc.). Group logos often include some letters. Lettering creates a formal, "businesslike" effect which may or may not be appropriate for your flag.

Sketch your proposed design with and without lettering. If letters or words are desired, abbreviate or just use initials. A single very large letter, or 2 or 3, can be an excellent basis for a design.

For ease of sewing, choose extra-bold sans-serif letters with clean straight lines and broad strokes. Computer word-processing programs and drawing programs usually include plain and ornamental typefaces that can be enlarged to fit on your flag. If you do not have access to a computer, clip-art alphabet books are readily available. (See Resource Guide on page 24.)

To judge appropriate size, sketch letters full-scale and stand back a distance that approximates how the flag will be viewed. It will become quite obvious whether the text is readable or not.

Front   Back

"MOM" reads the same forwards and backwards, but most words are confusing when reversed. Turn to pages 18 and 19 for practical ideas for incorporating graphics with text or other directional elements.

A single letter is easily recognized when seen reversed.

Try arcs or diagonal arrangements of letters.

GENERAL RULES for VIEWING DISTANCE (Extra-bold type)

To be legible at this distance:	Letters should be at least:
25 feet	2 - 2 ½ inches high
50 feet	3 - 3 ½ inches high
100 feet	4 - 5 inches high

PREPARE A PAPER PATTERN

Once your flag design and layout is finalized, you will need to create a **full-size** paper pattern from which to work. This is your Flag Plan. It should have clear, bold outlines of all design elements and include allowances for hems and casings.

Enlarge the Image

Any one of the following methods can be used to enlarge a small drawing or illustration to full-flag size:

★ Enlarge the drawing section by section on a self-service photocopier and tape the resulting pages together.

★ Take the drawing to a copy shop that has a large-format copier. Request that your design be enlarged to the desired size.

★ If the flag drawing was created on (or scanned into) a computer, print out enlarged design section by section on standard printer paper that can then be taped together.

★ Use an overhead, opaque or slide projector to project the image onto a large piece of paper; trace the outlines with a pencil.

★ Use the classic Grid Method of enlarging one square at a time:
    1. Sketch your design on graph paper and let each grid square represent X on the enlarged design.
    2. Draw a corresponding full-size grid on a large sheet of paper. Referring to the small drawing, sketch in lines of the design square by square on the larger sheet.

When you are satisfied with your design and layout, darken the outlines of all design elements with a felt-tip marker to make them easier to trace onto the flag fabric. To help avoid confusion during flag assembly, assign a "color code" (A, B, etc.) to each accent color you intend to use. First, identify whichever color covers the largest area in the design as "A." Color "B" will be the color that covers the next largest area, and so on. For reference, cut out a small swatch of each accent color, label it with its color code with a marker or adhesive label, and tape it onto the paper pattern. Next, clearly label <u>every</u> section of your design with its color code. If you wish, fill in the colors using colored pencils or

What kind of paper?
Graph paper may be helpful for making sketches and is ideal if you choose to enlarge your design with the "grid" method. To make a full-size paper pattern, extra-wide paper is available at art or drafting supplies stores. Or, tape 8½" x 11" sheets together to obtain whatever size you need.

Grid Method of Enlarging

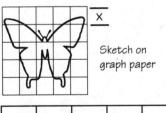

Sketch on graph paper

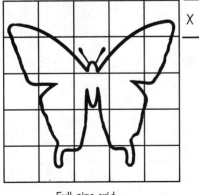

Full-size grid

markers. Finally, mark grain direction with a lengthwise double-ended arrow (see FLAGMAKER'S TIP about grain direction on page 16).

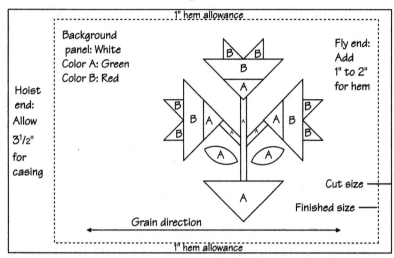

Flag Plan

Cut size of the main panel is slightly larger than the **finished size** of the flag because it includes allowances for hems and casing. Add the following allowances to the finished size of your flag:
- ★ Long-edge hems: 1" on each side
- ★ Fly hem: 1" (1½"- 2", if flag is longer than 5')
- ★ Hoist casing: 3½" (wider if the flag pole is over 1" in diameter)

Figure Yardage

Once you have finished your full-size paper pattern or Flag Plan, you can determine how large a piece of fabric you will need for each color in the design. (Take your paper Flag Plan with you when you go shopping.)

The **background panel** will be the largest piece. You will need a piece of fabric the full finished size of the flag plus allowances for hems and casings. (<u>Or</u>, buy a prehemmed Flag Blank. See page 10.)

For each **accent color,** you will need a piece of fabric big enough to cover all the sections in your design that appear in that color. For example, fabric purchased for the butterfly at the right has to entirely cover A-coded sections, plus 2" more in width and height just to be safe. The same applies to subsequent colors B, C, etc. If a color is used in small sections that are spread far apart in the design, to save fabric, you can place separate smaller pieces where needed.

NOTE: If you want grommets in the hoist end of the flag instead of a pole casing, see page 20.

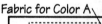

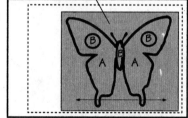

FLAGMAKER'S TIP: For best results, the "grain" direction of all the pieces used in the project should be oriented the same way. (See page 16.)

MAKE YOUR OWN Outdoor Flags & Banners

Streamers made of polyester, nylon, or satin ribbons add pizzazz to decorative flags.

Anchor tab (actual size): Lightweight leather, 1/16"-thick or less. Hole in tab fits over screw or fitting on flag pole.

The anchor tab may not be necessary if the flag will hang straight down (as from a dowel or curtain rod) or if the method of display requires grommets.

MATERIALS, SUPPLIES AND TOOLS

★ FLAG BLANK: Plain solid-color flags in standard sizes can be purchased from flag stores and catalogs. Called "blanks," they come pre-hemmed with grommets or pole casings in place. Lacking any decoration, they are a blank slate for original designs. Sizes and colors are limited, though, and may not fit your Flag Plan.

★ FABRIC: Commercial-quality, 200 denier (pronounced **den**-yer) **nylon flag oxford** is preferred for use outdoors because it is weather resistant, dries quickly and retains its strength when wet. A built-in UV stabilizer provides resistance to fading and deterioration caused by exposure to sunlight. This fabric is very strong for its weight and affords a better balance of flyablity, durability and economy than natural fibers or lighter- or heavier-weight nylons. It comes 60" wide and is available in dozens of beautiful, translucent colors. Completely reversible, with no "right" or "wrong" side, it does not need pre-washing. To store, wrap yardage and scraps on cardboard tubes. (Coated nylons are less appropriate for background panels since the fabric is heavier and the coating tends to drag against the bed of the sewing machine during stitching, but they can be used for Plain Appliqué.)

★ THREAD: Zigzag sewing requires lots of thread. Good quality (name-brand) **100% polyester thread** produces the best-looking stitching. Other types of threads such as rayon or cotton are less durable if exposed to the elements, and may not make as nice a stitch. Allow two or three 250- to 300-yard spools of thread per average 3' x 5' flag.

★ ANCHOR TABS: An anchor tab is a 2" x 1/2" strip of lightweight leather that has a small hole punched in one end. It is stitched into the flag's pole casing before it is sewn closed. When installing the completed flag on a flagpole, the tab can be slipped over a fitting or screw on the flagpole to keep the flag in place. To make your own "tab" from nylon oxford or grosgrain ribbon, see page 13.

★ STABILIZER: To improve stitch quality, treat nylon fabric with spray starch, sizing, water-soluble liquid or spray stabilizer at any time prior to sewing. These add body to the material, yet can be readily rinsed out once you are finished sewing. We do not recommend the use of tear-away stabilizer since stitching is stressed during removal and a messy residue is left behind.

★ LIGHTWEIGHT FUSIBLE WEB: In the Plain Appliqué method described on page 18, this product is used to position cut-out shapes on the flag prior to sewing.

★ SEWING MACHINE: Nothing fancy, just an ordinary machine with a zigzag stitch. Thread tension regulators and feed mnisms should be in good working order.

★ NEEDLE: For all sewing use a #12 or #14 ne Sharp). A new needle can sometimes mak the quality of your stitching.

★ RULER : A 24" x 6" plastic rotary cutting size, but any straightedge will do.

★ PENCILS : A #2 lead pencil is fine for most marking on fabric. A light- or silver-colored pencil shows up best on dark colors.

★ SCISSORS: For cutting out the background panel and accent colors prior to appliqué, use a rotary cutter and cutting mat or a sharp pair of 7" or 8" shears. For neatly trimming appliquéd sections, use a 5" pair that has very sharp, pointed tips or use appliqué scissors.

★ IRON & IRONING BOARD: For pressing nylon, use the lowest iron setting (Synthetics). High temperatures can cause nylon to buckle and even melt. A press cloth can help protect the flag in case the iron overheats. Steam is not produced at low settings, so mist fabric lightly with water before ironing.

★ PATTERN WEIGHTS: These keep your ruler and fabric pieces from sliding and shifting around as you work. If you wish, substitute river rocks, cans of soup or baby food jars filled with sand.

★ PINS: 1" or 1½" safety pins protect hands and arms from pin pricks during sewing. Otherwise, ordinary straight pins in good condition (sharp, smooth and straight) are fine.

..ne Foot?

CHING:
-purpose foot for all
 stitching: hems, seams,
 casings. It can also be used
 or appliqué stitching if you don't
have an appliqué foot.

ZIGZAG STITCHING
Test your stitching on a double layer of flag fabric with various presser feet, if you have them, to see which produces the most uniform zigzag stitching.

Appliqué foot

 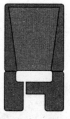

Top   Underside

• Use an **Appliqué foot** for uniform feed of the fabric during zigzag sewing. The indentation on the bottom surface of the appliqué foot allows zigzag thread "buildup" to glide freely underneath the foot.

• Try a **Walking foot** for either straight or zigzag stitching. It feeds the top layer of fabric at the same rate that the feed dogs advance the bottom layer.

2. MAKING THE FLAG

CONSTRUCT THE BACKGROUND PANEL

To make the background panel for a flag, follow the steps below.

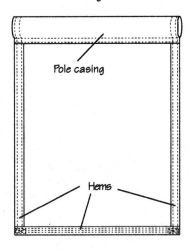

Finished Background Panel (Pole casing, Hems)

1. CUT OUT THE BACKGROUND PANEL: Position yardage for the background panel squarely on top of the paper Flag Plan. Trace the <u>outside cutting line</u> onto the fabric, and cut the background panel this size. The grain of the fabric should be parallel to two of the four edges of the flag. Use a rotary cutter and a long ruler to cut straight, very crisp edges

2. HEM THREE EDGES: The first sewing step is to finish the edges of the flag with hems to prevent them from fraying as you work. Make ½" hems on both long sides <u>and</u> the fly end of the background panel (fly end hem is wider if flag is large, see page 9). Crease the folds in the hem first, then topstitch.

   a. First Fold: Position your 24" ruler 2" from the raw edge of fabric. (Place pattern weights on the ruler to keep it from shifting as you work.) Next, fold the raw edge over so it butts up against the ruler. Press the fold in place with fingertips and then crease fold sharply with fingernail.

   b. Second Fold: Put your ruler aside and repeat the process, this time folding the same raw edge over so that it butts up to the first fold. Finger press in place, then crease firmly.

   c. Fold both folds over so hem is flat and raw edge is enclosed. Pin liberally: every 4" to 5" or so.

   d. Topstitch hem using a straight stitch (12-15 stitches per inch). Stitch ⅛" from fold on inside edge of hem, anchoring threads by backtacking ½" at beginning and end of hem. Add a second row of stitching ⅛" from fold on outside edge of hem. After stitching both sides of the flag, hem the fly end in the same manner.

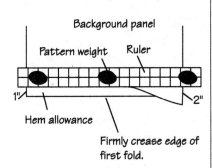

Folding Hems (Background panel, Pattern weight, Ruler, 1", 2", Hem allowance, Firmly crease edge of first fold.)

FLAGMAKER'S TIP: Although nylon oxford has no right or wrong side, the yardage has a distinct curve when it comes off the roll. To take advantage of this natural curl, position fabric with curl facing up when creasing hems.

3. MAKE A POLE CASING: On the remaining unhemmed side of the flag panel (the hoist end), fold the raw edge of the fabric over $3\frac{1}{2}$" and crease. Then fold the same edge over just $\frac{1}{2}$" and crease firmly. (Note: If your flagpole is over 1" in diameter, make the pole casing a bit wider. See page 9.)

Anchor Tabs: Before topstitching the pole casing, add an anchor tab for attaching the flag to the flag pole. (See page 10.) For upright or diagonally mounted flags, determine which end of the casing will be "up" when the flag is on display, and position the tab at this end of pole casing. Centering over the first crease, $3\frac{1}{2}$" from raw edge, sew tab to flag with "box-X" stitching (see illustration this page) leaving slit end of tab free. A special-sized needle for stitching leather may be needed if leather is thick or machine lacks gumption.

To topstitch casing, refold, then pin closed and topstitch along the inside edge; backtack $\frac{1}{2}$" at beginning and end of stitching. For extra durability, reinforce with a second row of stitching $\frac{1}{4}$" from first row.

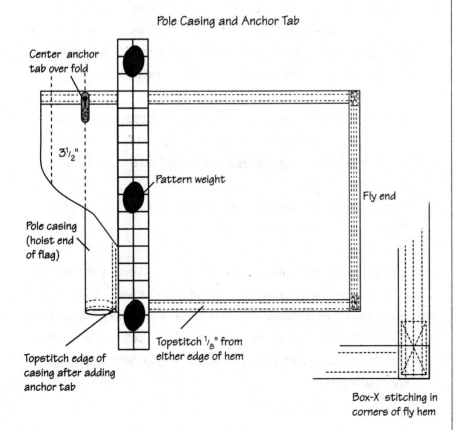

Pole Casing and Anchor Tab

Make Your Own Anchor Tab

A scrap of nylon oxford can be fashioned into a workable substitute for leather.

- Cut a $1\frac{1}{2}$" X $4\frac{1}{2}$" strip of nylon. Match the color to the background panel of the flag.
- Fold in thirds lengthwise and topstitch the long edges using two rows of topstitching $\frac{1}{4}$" apart.

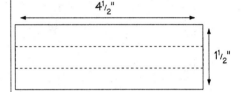

- Fold one end under $\frac{1}{2}$" and pin; fold the other end $1\frac{3}{4}$" under and pin so that the tab measures $\frac{1}{2}$" x $2\frac{1}{4}$". Stitch free ends down.

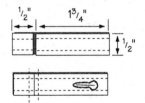

- Make a $\frac{1}{2}$"-long buttonhole $\frac{3}{8}$" from one end. Cut buttonhole open.

FLAGMAKER'S TIP: The hem at the free-flying end of a flag is vulnerable to tattering caused by wind and weather. Strengthen this hem by adding a third row of stitching between the other rows. Add Box-X reinforcement stitching to both corners.

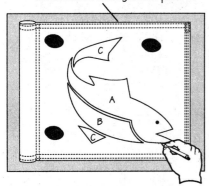

Place full-size paper Flag Plan underneath background panel

Trace all pattern lines and symbols onto front of flag. Hold layers still with pattern weights or tape.

TRANSFER THE DESIGN OUTLINES

Position hemmed background panel right side up over the paper Flag Plan, and trace the major lines of the entire design directly onto the fabric. If the background panel is light-colored, the lines of the design will be clearly visible. If the fabric color is too dark to see through, place the pattern and flag over a light table or tape them onto a window.

Using a #2 or a colored pencil and a ruler for straight lines (if any), accurately trace <u>all</u> pattern outlines and color-code symbols directly onto the front side of the flag. For best visibility, make distinct, conspicuous marks (zigzag stitching will conceal all but the darkest marks). Color-code symbols will help you keep track of which sections to stitch and trim and will automatically be removed later during trimming. Use pattern weights, pins or tape to keep the layers from shifting as you work.

SET UP MACHINE FOR ZIGZAG STITCHING

Since the strength and integrity of the entire flag depends ultimately on relatively narrow stitching, it is important to set up the sewing machine to produce a good, strong zigzag stitch.

★ Change presser foot to either a plain zigzag or appliqué foot.

★ Use the same color thread in the bobbin as on top. If your machine can produce perfectly-balanced tension, you can use a contrasting color in the bobbin if you wish.

★ **Set zigzag stitch WIDTH to no less than 1/8" (3mm) and no more than 3/16" (4.5mm).** If it is too wide, the weave of the fabric tends to get pinched, distorting the design. **Set stitch LENGTH so that you are able to glimpse some of the underlying fabric between each stitch.** It should be short enough to prevent fraying, but long enough to be fast and forgiving. By using this "extended" satin stitch rather than a solid satin stitch, problems with thread buildup are minimized and little, if any, seam strength is sacrificed.

The Stitch
Recommended stitch width and length for extended satin stitch

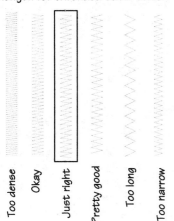

Too dense · Okay · Just right · Pretty good · Too long · Too narrow

MAKE YOUR OWN Outdoor Flags & Banners

> **Machine Readiness Checklist**
> **ZIGZAG STITCH:**
>   Width: 1/8"- 3/16" (3-4.5mm)
>   Length: 30-40 stitches per inch
> **FOOT:** Appliqué, plain zigzag or walking foot
> **NEEDLE:** #12 or #14 Universal or Sharp
> **THREAD:** 100 % Polyester (name brand)
> **TENSION:** Top thread loosened slightly

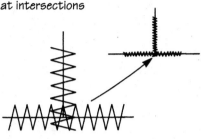

Diagram A: Overlap and backtack at intersections

★ Experiment with thread tension, stitch width and length on a test swatch of <u>two layers</u> of fabric until you get an attractive stitch on both sides of the fabric. Practice stitching corners and curves. For uniform stitches, let the machine feed at its own pace, without trying to push or pull the fabric through. If necessary for balanced tension, ease up on the top thread tension. Refer to your sewing machine manual for details.

★ Practice stitching in these specific situations before you start on your actual flag:

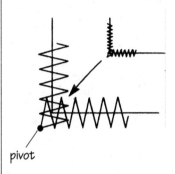

Diagram B: Corners

- OVERLAPS AND BACKTACKS: When completing a sewn circuit, stitch past the starting point, securely overlapping stitches by at least 1/2". Be sure to include 1/4" to 1/2" backtacks at the beginning and ending of every line of stitching.

- INTERSECTIONS: When a corner or a line intersects another line of stitching, sew past the intersection a distance no more than half the width of the zigzag stitch, about 1/16" (Diagram A).

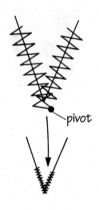

Diagram C: Acute-angle corners

- CORNERS: For a neat, secure corner, sew just past the corner, stopping with the needle in the fabric (Diagram B). Raise the presser foot, pivot, lower the foot and resume sewing. On acute-angle corners, the point will be slightly squared off (Diagram C).

- CURVES: Steer around shallow curves at a steady, moderate rate. For sharp curves, hand-walk machine, pivoting slightly on the inside (or outside) of the curve every few stitches for a uniform fanlike effect (Diagram D). Setting the presser foot somewhat lighter than normal can be a big advantage in this situation.

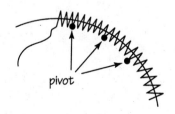

Diagram D: Curves

TO PIVOT: Leave needle in fabric and then raise presser foot.

MAKE YOUR OWN Outdoor Flags & Banners

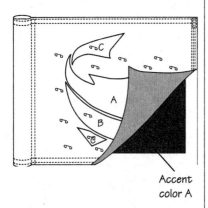
Accent color A

REVERSIBLE APPLIQUÉ

Reversible Appliqué allows you to produce a design on both sides of the flag at once. With this method you will layer, stitch and trim one color of the design at a time.

1. LAYER: Referring to your paper Flag Plan, determine which accent color is to be added first (usually the color occupying the greatest area of the design). This color will be designated "A." Cut one piece of accent fabric A large enough to cover all the sections marked A, plus <u>at least</u> 1/2" all around. (This "gripper" will give you something substantial to hold onto later during trimming.) Make sure grain direction is oriented correctly before you cut into the fabric.

Place the piece of accent fabric A on the table first, then position the background panel of the flag on top of it, <u>right side up</u>. Adjust so that accent fabric A is under every A section. Using lots of safety pins or straight pins, pin-baste the two layers together. Avoiding pattern lines, pin every 3", including areas outside of the design.

FLAGMAKER'S TIP: The direction of the yarns in woven fabric is called the **GRAIN**. "Straight" grain runs parallel to the selvedge (woven edge) of the fabric. **Where possible, match the straight grain direction of all layers of the project.** If you rotate any of the pieces in an attempt to use yardage more efficiently, it may pucker when sewn and distort the design and drape of the flag.

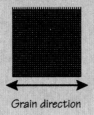
Grain direction

2. STITCH: All zigzag appliqué sewing is done with the flag right-side up so pencil marks are easy to see. Locate all sections marked with an A, and zigzag around the perimeter of each one. Center stitching directly over pencil marks. Before starting, take a moment to plan your sewing route so as to connect lines of stitching in continuous "circuits" where possible. Generally, start at the center and work outwards so that the bulk of the fabric remains to the left of the needle as much as possible.

During sewing, bundle or "package" the flag by loosely rolling and folding each edge, so that the flag readily fits under the head of the sewing machine. As you progress, re-roll to expose various parts of the design. The flag should be well supported. An extension table surrounding the bed of the sewing machine is ideal to keep the area to be stitched flat, smooth and free to move.

After sewing completely around all A sections, remove pins, pull thread tails to wrong side and clip.

TROUBLESHOOTING: For stitching that does not pass muster:
1) Re-thread machine.
2) Try appliqué or walking foot.
3) Adjust top and/or bottom tension.
4) Replace needle.
5) Try different thread (upgrade).
6) Adjust stitch length or width slightly.
7) Adjust presser foot pressure.
8) Try stabilizer or starch.

3. TRIM: In this two-part step, the entire flag will be reduced to one layer as you trim away unneeded fabric - first on the front, then the back - to reveal the design on both sides of the flag.

First, position flag right side up. Place a "reference" pin in every section of the design that has a color code <u>other</u> than A. The pins will serve as a visual cue to help prevent you from accidentally trimming away design sections that should remain intact.

Next, pinch and separate layers. Choose any A (unpinned) section. Using both hands, one underneath and one on top, grasp fabric layers between thumb and fingers to separate the top and bottom layers. Poke the point of a pair of small sharp scissors into the top layer to make a slit. Carefully trim away the top layer of fabric, as close to the stitching as possible, all around the inside perimeter of the section. (TIP: For neatest trimming, angle the blades of the scissors flat against the fabric.) As trimming proceeds, be very careful <u>not</u> to cut into sections in which you have placed reference pins. Take care to avoid cutting into stitching or the underlying fabric. Repeat on all remaining A (unpinned) sections on front side of flag. When finished, remove all reference pins before starting to trim on reverse side of the flag.

TRIMMING TIP: Once you get the hang of it, it is possible to trim close enough to the stitching so that when you are finished, it can be hard to tell the difference between the front and the back.

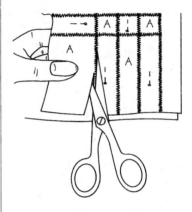

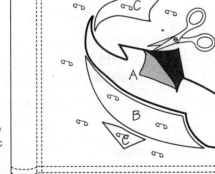

Stitch around sections marked A, and then trim away only the top layer to expose accent fabric A underneath.

FIX-IT TIP: If you inadvertently cut any stitches, dab with Fray Check™ or any other fast-drying permanent glue, then re-stitch. If you accidentally cut into the wrong layer of fabric, you can repair it by patching in from underneath with a matching scrap of fabric, using the same Layer-Stitch-Trim method.

Finally, to trim the design on the reverse side of the flag, turn it over so the reverse side faces up. Place reference pins in all sections that are a <u>single layer</u> of fabric. Now, trim away the top layer only of all <u>two-layer</u> (unpinned) sections to reveal the underlying, background panel color. When you are finished, the entire flag will be one layer.

SEWING TIP: For easier "tracking" during sewing, draw a visual reference mark on the center of your presser foot with a fine-tipped marker or piece of tape. Watch the reference mark, not the needle, as you sew along the traced lines.

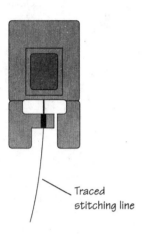

COVER PATCH: To make text "read right" on both sides of the flag, appliqué letters onto a cover patch for the back side. Then, appliqué patch onto flag with a zigzag stitch and trim away excess fabric around the outside of stitching.

Front

Back

NOTE: Depending on your flag design, you may have just removed some A sections that were also marked with "B" (or "C," "D," etc.), indicating sections to be sewn in those colors. In that case, position flag over the paper pattern again and retrace any missing lines and letters.

4. ADD REMAINING COLORS: In this step, you will add accent fabric B to your flag design, continuing with the same Layer-Stitch-Trim method. If your design involves additional colors, repeat this process for each color, in alphabetical order, until all colors have been added and design is complete.

a. LAYER: Position the flag right side up over accent fabric B; securely pin-baste layers together.

b. STITCH: Zigzag around the entire perimeter of all sections marked B. In some places, your stitching may overlap previous stitching.

c. TRIM: Trim to reveal color B following the steps described on page 17 for color A.

APPLIQUÉ LETTERS AND NUMBERS

Letters and other small design details are usually added last. We use Plain Appliqué for letters and directional motifs. In this method fabric letters or other design elements are cut out and then stitched to the flag background. This produces a double layer of fabric which makes the flag heavier than the Reversible Appliqué method. The letters will appear only on the front of the flag. If any part of your emblem or lettering is directional <u>and</u> you want it to "read right" on both sides of your flag, cut out two complete sets of letters or other design elements. Appliqué the first set onto the front of your flag. Then, appliqué the other set onto an appropriately-sized cover patch that matches the color of the background panel. Then stitch this patch onto the reverse side of the flag in the appropriate place in the layout.

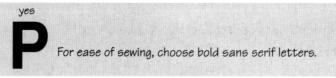

For ease of sewing, choose bold sans serif letters.

★ One option is to use ready-made iron-on letters. Iron-on letters do not need to be sewn for onetime or indoor uses: just place them in position, press down with the iron (at the coolest setting), and you are done!

★ You can make your own "iron-on" letters, numbers or other directional motifs with a lightweight paper-backed fusible web product. Follow the steps below for Plain Appliqué.

1. Transfer letter outlines to the fabric. Draw or photo-copy letters full-size onto a piece of plain paper. Rub chalk onto the back of the paper. (Use a contrasting color that will show up on your letter fabric.) Place fabric right side up on work surface. Position paper over the fabric, chalk side down, and trace firmly around the edge of each letter with a sharp pencil or ball-point pen. (Carbon paper can be used in place of chalk.)

2. Fuse the web to the fabric. Position rough side of lightweight paper-backed fusible web against the wrong side of the lettering fabric. To help protect fabric from heat, place a press cloth over the area to be fused. With a dry iron set on "medium," press firmly, without moving iron, for approximately 5 seconds. Repeat over entire area to be fused. (Check product directions first.)

3. Cut letters out. For "cleanest" effect, use an X-Acto® knife and ruler to guide cutting on the straight sides of letters.

4. Make a guide for arranging letters in a straight line. Fold and crease flag (or cover patch) lightly, or tape a piece of thread in the appropriate place.

5. Fuse letters onto flag. Remove paper backing from fusible web side of letters. Position letters on flag, fusible side down. Place a press cloth over the area to be fused, and fuse as in step 2 above. **Important! Nylon is more sensitive to heat than most fabrics. Experiment first on scraps to determine the right amount of heat and pressure.**

6. Stitch around each letter with a zigzag stitch for a durable, washable finish (see page 14). Match thread to letter color.

FLAGMAKER'S TIP: Letters look more precise if they are cut out first, then stitched to the flag. To avoid shifting and bunching up, glue, fuse or pin letters securely before stitching.

Transferring letter outlines to the fabric

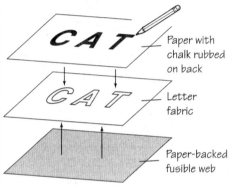

Paper with chalk rubbed on back
Letter fabric
Paper-backed fusible web

FLAGMAKER'S TIP: Although coated 200- or 400-denier nylon may be too heavy for the background panel of a flag, it can be easier to use for Plain Appliqué because it is more stable than uncoated nylon.

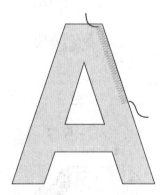

SEWING TIP: To attach letters securely, align edge of zigzag stitching with edge of letter.

HEADINGS AND GROMMETS

If the method for displaying the flag requires grommets (see Halyards on page 22), the hoist end will need a "heading," a sturdy binding that reinforces the edge where grommets are inserted, instead of a pole casing. Both fabric and webbing are suitable.

★ FABRIC HEADING: Cut a piece of 200-denier nylon fabric four times the finished heading width, typically 1" to 2", and 4" longer than the hoist end of your flag. Fold and press it lengthwise, open it back out, and turn the ends in toward the center 2". Finally, fold each long edge in all the way to the center fold, and fold back in half, resulting in a heading that is four layers thick throughout, except at the ends where there are 8 layers. Slip your flag evenly into the heading, pin securely, and sew around all four edges of the heading, using a straight or zigzag stitch.

★ WEBBING HEADING (nylon, polyester, or polypropylene): Cut 1"- to 2"-wide woven webbing twice as long as the hoist end measurement, plus 3" for overlap. Finish cut ends with a zigzag stitch, a hotknife or candle flame. Since the webbing is usually too thick for pinning, attach it to the edge of the flag with double-sided tape prior to topstitching. Topstitch as described above.

★ GROMMETS: You can buy inexpensive kits with the tools and materials needed to insert lightweight sheet-metal grommets in your flag heading. However, these lightweight grommets are not really strong enough for flags exposed to wind and weather. If your flag will get particularly hard use, ask an awning company or sailmaker to install heavy-duty "spur" grommets for you. Often the cost of this service is very small.

FINISHING TOUCHES

★ Hang up your flag and view it from several feet away to decide how much you want to worry about remaining stray frizzy fibers leftover from trimming. Trim as needed.

★ Add machine-stitched embellishments such as fine embroidered lettering and accent stitching as desired.

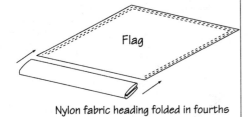

Fabric Heading

Nylon fabric heading folded in fourths lenghtwise

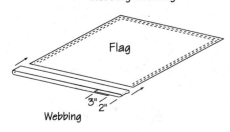

Webbing Heading

Webbing

For Your New House!
1996 from Susan M.

To commemorate an event or occasion, add a label featuring your name and a date. Use an indelible ink pen to write on a piece of fabric, write directly on the heading or hem, or embroider this detail.

3. FLAG DISPLAY & CARE

FLAG DISPLAY

Nylon flags are ideal for outdoor use, but are perfectly appropriate for indoor display as well. Placed in a window, the colors glow like stained glass in the sunlight. Mount your flag in a window frame by inserting a spring-loaded curtain rod or dowel through the pole casing. Or just pin it to a wall or ceiling beam with push pins.

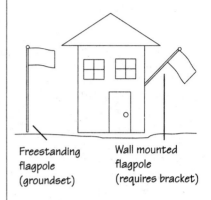

Freestanding flagpole (groundset)

Wall mounted flagpole (requires bracket)

Outside, flags will catch the light <u>and</u> the wind, adding movement to the equation. Turrets, gazebos, greenhouses and mailboxes all provide opportunities to display flags. And do not forget decks, patios, the summer cabin, boats and docks. Flags are also great for parades, picnics, and team sporting events. Most outdoor display situations require some sort of flagpole and bracket. (See Resource Guide on page 24.)

★ FLAGPOLES: Flagpoles can be either groundset in an upright position or wall-mounted at an angle on a building or other structure. Groundset poles are available in convenient 2- or 3-piece sectional kits for do-it-yourselfers. Unless the flag is fairly small, it may be necessary to obtain a display permit in your town or neighborhood. Ask a flagpole dealer or check local regulations for height restrictions.

Fiberglass poles may be the best choice for permanent display: wood is not as strong and may warp and splinter when used outside. Light-gauge aluminum can bend and grayish aluminum oxide rubs off on fabric.

★ BRACKETS: Several kinds of brackets are available. Our favorite, the adjustable kind, can be mounted on either a vertical or horizontal surface and can be adjusted to display flags at any of several angles.

DISPLAY TIP: The rule of thumb for determining flagpole height for a residence is that it should be roughly as tall as or slightly taller than the house, approximately 12 feet per floor. The flag length should be about one fourth the height of the pole.

In the US, flag etiquette dictates that any flag flown together with the American flag is respectfully flown in a lower (subordinate) position, whether it is on the same or an adjacent flagpole, and likewise should be smaller in size. Consult a flag or flagpole dealer for recommendations for your specific situation.

Adjustable flag bracket

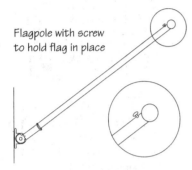

Flagpole with screw to hold flag in place

Garden flag bracket

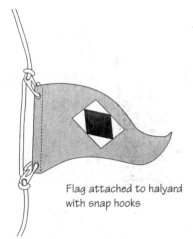

Flag attached to halyard with snap hooks

★ ANTI-FURLING DEVICES: Flags displayed from horizontal or diagonally-mounted flagpoles have a maddening tendency to wrap, or "furl," themselves around the pole and stay that way until someone gets a ladder out and unwraps them. Several types of devices are available to eliminate this problem. One is a plastic sleeve that fits over a flagpole. The flag's pole casing fits over this plastic tube, and both rotate around the pole in the wind. Another device features two or more plastic cylindrical bearings that rotate at a fixed point on the pole. The flag is attached to the bearings with snap hooks. These devices are not foolproof, but they seem to be better than nothing.

NOTE: Diagonal- or vertical-mount flagpoles need an anchoring device near the top to hold the flag in place. This feature is built into most anti-furling devices. If not, insert a short screw most of the way into a wooden pole. The anchor tab described on page 10 fits over the screw to secure the flag to the pole. Alternatively, thread a removable cable tie (available at hardware stores and home centers) through the slit in the anchor tab and tighten securely around the pole.

★ SPECIALTY BRACKETS: Garden flag brackets are especially fun for small flags that have been designed to hang straight down. These metal stands can be stuck almost anywhere in the ground, or in flower pots or planters. Special brackets designed to mount on mailboxes are also available.

★ HALYARDS: A halyard is a line on a flagpole or mast for hoisting the flag into place. It is fitted with snap hooks or other fasteners which attach to the grommets on a flag. Commercially-made national and state flags are bound and reinforced on the hoist end with rugged fabric or synthetic webbing that supports heavy duty grommets. This is the preferred finish for large flags (4' x 6' plus) and flags that will receive heavy wear. For directions on adding a heading and grommets to your flag, see page 20.

FLAG CARE

★ DISPLAY TIPS: For longest wear, remove the flag from display during strong winds. Prolonged periods of lively flapping will blow out seams and hems, particularly if fabric has been weakened from long exposure to the sun. Likewise, if possible, hang the flag in a spot where it is not exposed to the strongest midday sun and where it will not flap repeatedly against a building or shrubbery. The first signs of wear are likely to be along the free-flying end. Over time, fluttering and flapping causes disintegration of fibers and thread that are already weakened by exposure to the sun.

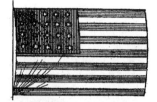

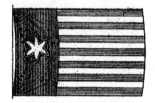

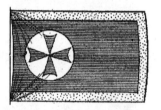

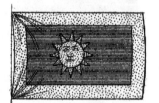

★ REPAIR: Inspect your flag periodically for signs of wear and repair any deteriorating stitching. If necessary, re-hem or patch tattered areas. Use the same sewing techniques described on pages 12 through 18.

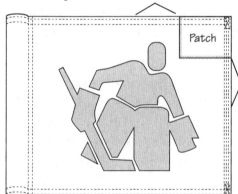

HINT: Open several inches of topstitching in hems before applying patch. Then re-stitch hems along with patch hems.

★ WASHING: Machine or hand wash in cold or warm water with any mild detergent. Do not use bleach. Protect stitching from snagging by placing the flag in a zippered mesh bag.

IMPORTANT! **Do not put a nylon flag in the dryer**. Line dry away from heat. Press with a dry iron on lowest setting (350 degrees tops - anything higher risks glazing or melting) Mist with water for smoother ironing.

★ STORING: Be sure the flag is clean and dry before placing in storage. To store, fold or roll on a cardboard tube, or hang over a dowel or rack suspended from the ceiling in a closet, basement, attic, garage, etc.

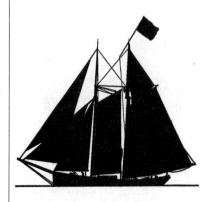

RESOURCE GUIDE

Flag Publications:
Banners and Hangings, Laliberté & McIlhany. Reinhold, 1966
Flags, Kent Alexander. Mallard Press, 1992
Flags of the World, edited by Barraclough & Crampton. F. Warne, 1978
Flags Through the Ages and Across the World, Whitney Smith. McGraw-Hill, 1975
The Oxford Guide to Heraldry, Woodcock & Robinson. Oxford University Press, 1988
The Stars and the Stripes, Boleslaw Mastai. Knopf, 1973

For Flag Buffs:
The Flag Research Center
Dr. Whitney Smith, Director
PO Box 580
Winchester, MA 01890
Phone: (617) 729-9410
Flag documentation and consulting services; outstanding selection of current vexillological publications including The Flag Bulletin, bimonthly journal ($40/yr.).

North American Vexillological Association
1977 N. Olden Ave., Suite 225
Trenton, NJ 08618
Non-profit organization dedicated to the promotion of the scientific and scholarly study of flag history and symbolism (vexillology). Membership open to any interested individual (annual dues $18).

Flag Design:
A Flag for New Milford, Peter J. Orenski. The Flag Bulletin #168, (1996), published by The Flag Research Center (address above). A practical handbook on creating a successful civic flag ($10 ppd.).

Clip-Art:
Outline Alphabets: 100 Complete Fonts, Dan X. Solo. Dover, 1988. Elegant clip-art alphabets appropriate for flags. Dover's extensive offering of inexpensive clip-art books are available at bookstores; write for free Pictorial Archive Series catalogs:
Dover Publications, Inc.
31 East 2nd St.
Mineola, NY 11501

DeskGallery: Mega-Bundle
Clip-Art on CD-ROM for Macintosh® and Windows® from the Dover Electronic Pictorial Design Series.
Zedcor, Inc.
3420 N. Dodge Blvd. Suite Z
Tucson, AZ 85716
Internet: zedcor@zedcor.com

Graphics Supplies:
ArtGrafix
15 Tech Circle
Natick, MA 01760
Phone: (800) 443-4421
Discount graphics and artist supplies. Free mail-order catalog.

Fabric, Supplies, Flagpoles & Hardware:
KarLin of Quakertown
420 East Broad Street
Quakertown, PA 18951
Phone: (800) 828-7798
Complete selection of flag- and banner-making materials and supplies, flagpoles and display hardware. Free informative mail-order catalog/newsletter.

Central Coast Creations
PO Box 3643
San Luis Obispo, CA 93403
Phone: (805) 466-9379
Flag- and banner-making materials and supplies; flagpoles and display hardware. Mail-order catalog ($1).

Funtastic Flags
PO Box 15122
Charlotte, NC 28211
Phone: (888) FUN-FLAG
Flag- and banner-making materials and supplies. Mail-order catalog ($2 plus S.A.S.E.).

The Flag Works
1421 Montgomery Road
Allison Park, PA 15101
Phone: (412) 364-5780
Flag- and banner-making materials and supplies; flagpoles and display hardware. Mail-order catalog ($1).

Goodwind's Kites
3333 Wallingford Ave. N.
Seattle, WA 98103
Phone: (206) 632-6151
Flag- and banner-making materials and supplies, hard-to-find parts and the best tools, fittings and notions. Illustrated, informative mail-order catalog ($5.00, or available free at kite stores).

Kite Studio
5555 Hamilton Blvd.
Wescosville, PA 18106
Phone: (610) 395-3560
Flag- and banner-making supplies. Free mail-order catalog.

The Rain Shed
707 NW 11th
Corvallis, OR 97330
Phone: (503) 753-8900
"Recreational" fabrics, including flag- and banner-making materials and supplies. Free illustrated mail-order catalog.

Seattle Fabrics
8702 Aurora Ave. N.
Seattle, WA 98103
Phone: (206) 632-6022
"Recreational" fabrics, including flag- and banner-making materials and supplies. Mail order catalog ($3.00).

Elmer's Flag and Banner
1332 NE Broadway
Portland, OR 97232
Phone: (800) 547-8795
Ready-made US, state and foreign flags; flagpoles and display hardware. Free illustrated mail-order catalog.

The Flag Shop
1755 West 4th Ave.
Vancouver, BC V6J 1M2
Canada
Phone: (800) 663-8681
Ready-made state and foreign flags; flagpoles and display hardware. Free illustrated mail-order catalog. Also: "The Flag and Banner," informative general-interest newsletter published twice per year ($7.00 US for 4 issues).

Clotilde, Inc.
2 Sew Smart Way B8031
Stevens Point, WI 54481
Phone: (800) 772-2891
Complete line of discount sewing notions and supplies. Free mail order catalog.

Nancy's Notions Catalog
Box 683
Beaver Dam, WI 53916
Phone: (800) 833-0690
Complete line of discount sewing notions and supplies. Free mail order catalog.

ALSO: Refer to Yellow Pages listings under Flags & Flagpoles, Kite Stores, Home Centers, Awning Companies, Sailmakers, Artist Supplies.